21st Century Skills **INNOVATION** *Library*

Trains

by Katie Marsico

Published in the United States of America by Cherry Lake Publishing
Ann Arbor, Michigan
www.cherrylakepublishing.com

Content Adviser: Amy C. Newman, Director, Forney Museum of Transportation

Design: The Design Lab

Photo Credits: Cover and page 3, ©hfng, used under license from Shutterstock, Inc.; page 4,
©tbradford, used under license from Shutterstock, Inc.; pages 5 and 8, ©Mary Evans Picture
Library/Alamy; page 7, ©Graeme Knox, used under license from Shutterstock, Inc.; page 11,
©presse-bild-poss/Alamy; pages 13 and 28, ©North Wind Picture Archives/Alamy; pages 14, 17,
and 26, ©The Print Collector/Alamy; page 18, ©ClassicStock/Alamy; page 19, ©David R. Frazier
Photolibrary, Inc./Alamy; page 20, ©Lee Foster/Alamy; page 21, ©AP Photo/Katsumi Kasahara;
page 22, ©AP Photo/Eugene Hoshiko; page 25, ©Classic Image/Alamy

Library of Congress Cataloging-in-Publication Data
Marsico, Katie, 1980-
  Trains / by Katie Marsico.
     p. cm.–(Innovation in transportation)
  Includes index.
  ISBN-13: 978-1-60279-234-0
  ISBN-10: 1-60279-234-8
  1. Railroads–United States–History–Juvenile literature. I. Title. II. Series.

TF23.M35 2009
625.1–dc22   2008003204

*Cherry Lake Publishing would like to acknowledge the work of
The Partnership for 21st Century Skills.
Please visit www.21stcenturyskills.org for more information.*

CONTENTS

CHAPTER ONE

From Horses to 100-Car Giants

Many people ride the train to and from work.

You wait patiently at the station to hear the bellow of the train horn. You've aleady purchased your ticket. In a few minutes you will board the train and speed toward your destination. Your family owns a car, but who wants to be stuck in traffic all day? Besides, it's thrilling to sit and look out the window of a train as it chugs along. Maybe you'll even catch a glimpse of a long freight train running on a nearby track as it carries **cargo** across the country.

Before the invention of engine-powered vehicles, humans often relied on animals to transport goods and people.

No matter where you go or what you see when you ride the rails, you are taking advantage of a major innovation in transportation. Railroads and trains have shaped both society and history. Creative problem solvers developed trains as a way to move people and goods quickly from place to place. People continue to come up with new ideas every day about how to improve train technology.

Wooden railways were first laid in Europe starting in the 1500s. These wooden tracks were often called wagonways. Horses pulled wagons and flat carts carrying coal and salt along the tracks from mines to towns. The tracks allowed people to move goods between mines without having to rumble over bumpy, muddy roads and pathways. Horses and their drivers didn't have to spend as much **energy** dragging heavy loads across uneven ground.

As the years passed, businessmen and engineers pushed for even greater **efficiency**. They started laying iron rails in England in the late 1700s. The smooth metal cut down on the **friction** between wagon wheels and the ground. Eventually, innovations such as steam power and electricity drove massive **locomotives** along the tracks.

Today's trains can hardly be described as horse-drawn wagons. The average modern freight train is made up of 100 cars. It weighs 12 million to 20 million pounds (5.4 million to 9 million kilograms). These trains carry everything from coal to lumber to automobiles. Passenger trains run at ground level, on elevated platforms, and even underneath city streets. Like freight trains, most of these trains are powered by **fuel** and electricity.

So how did creative minds go from wooden tracks and horses to railway giants and passenger trains that clock in at more than 124 miles (200 km) per hour?

Businessmen, engineers, and everyday people all contributed to the creation of transportation that was faster and stronger than anything of the past.

Some creative thinkers realized that elevated trains could make the most of the limited space in crowded cities.

CHAPTER TWO

Building for Speed and Efficiency

The *Rocket* demonstrated the potential of the steam locomotive to the world.

The 1800s saw factories in England and the United States producing more goods than ever before. Horse-drawn wagons on rails worked well for 200 years. By the 1800s, however, businessmen in Europe and America needed to transport products and materials more quickly and in bigger quantities.

British inventor George Stephenson helped develop the technology that replaced animal power with the first steam locomotive. He relied heavily on the work of other inventors who had already come up with a device known as the steam engine. This engine used heat from burning coal or wood to boil water in a tank, creating steam. The steam was forced into cylinders. There it pushed pistons, which created the mechanical power that moved the train. Inventors struggled with developing a steam engine that would move heavy coal trains along railroads. Stephenson believed he could come up with a practical design.

In 1814, he designed his first steam locomotive. His vehicle had wheels, could pull other cars along railroad tracks, and was powered by a steam engine. The locomotive could haul 30 tons of coal uphill at a speed of 4 miles (6.4 km) per hour.

People also wanted a faster, more comfortable way to get from place to place. Riding in carriages over long distances could take days. It was often a bumpy, crowded experience. Travelers could journey in steamboats along rivers, but this was not always the most direct means of transportation.

Part of Stephenson's answer to these dilemmas was to design a locomotive that could be used to pull passenger trains. In about 1825, he managed to transport 450 people on the first passenger railway. The train traveled just less than 9 miles (14.5 km) at a speed of about 15 miles (24 km) per hour. Four years later, his

George Stephenson was a brilliant innovator, but he relied just as much on personal initiative as he did on creativity. This famous inventor was born to parents who could neither read nor write. His family was too poor to send him to school. Stephenson worked in a coal mine and saved enough money to attend night classes as a young adult. He took personal responsibility for his education. What he learned helped him to become a leader in the train industry.

Rocket transported both people and products at a speed of 36 miles (58 km) per hour—amazing for that period in history.

Though they were a great advance in technology, steam engines had their difficulties. Steam locomotives were made up of many detailed parts. Each part required frequent service and repair. Several workers were needed to operate each locomotive. Also, locomotives that chugged into major cities in both England and the United States belched out smoke, fumes, and soot. The engines burned coal to produce steam. The resulting pollution clouded train tunnels and the air near train stations in the late 1800s.

People trying to solve these problems had thought about using electricity to power trains since the 1830s. But finding a way to produce enough of this energy to transport people and products on a large scale over long distances was not easy. Then in the late 1800s, inventors discovered how to channel the power of electricity

The same fumes that pollute the environment can also be harmful to workers who inspect or repair trains.

into motors. They did this by using overhead electrical wires or electrified third rails. In 1895, the Baltimore and Ohio (B&O) Railroad became the first major railroad to successfully operate using electricity to power locomotives. This success led to the development of trolleys, subways, and modern commuter rails.

Power lines were expensive to build and maintain, so problem solvers continued trying to come up with even better ways to power trains. German inventor Rudolf Diesel was responsible for developing the diesel engine. The diesel engine runs on fuel that is made from heavy oil and that directly powers a train's locomotive.

Scientists took this knowledge a step further. They came up with a way to combine the diesel engine with electricity. They realized the diesel could power a device called a **generator**. In turn, the generator could produce electricity to turn motors that make a train's locomotive run. The result was the diesel-electric locomotive, which was first used on a passenger train in 1934. This type of locomotive was added to long-distance freight trains in 1941.

Diesel-electrics could haul more cargo than steam locomotives. They didn't require stops for water. That meant they could get more done in a shorter period of time. They required fewer repairs, and fewer workers were needed to run them. These reasons all led to the diesel-electric becoming the most common and popular model of locomotive on the rails today.

CHAPTER THREE

Expanding an Industry

Designing and creating the technology you have just read about required talent and determination. But engineers and scientists weren't the only ones who used these qualities to make trains an important part of modern society. Business leaders and politicians promoted the railroad. They pushed to spread tracks between communities and across entire countries.

Many immigrant workers helped contruct the Transcontinental Railroad.

The Transcontinental Railroad is an example of how such men and women supported railroad innovations. By the 1860s, the nation was expanding westward. Everyone from government leaders to ordinary people needed a rapid, reliable way to travel and ship goods across the country.

Stagecoaches and wagon trains could only haul so much so quickly. Their fastest wasn't fast enough to keep up with Americans' desire to be more connected citizens of an ever-larger country. The solution came when the government passed the Pacific Railway Act in 1862. This

In order to expand its railroad, the Central Pacific had to build tunnels through the Sierra Nevada mountains.

act legally supported the creation of the Transcontinental Railroad. It allowed the country to be linked by rail from coast to coast.

Both the U.S. government and private business leaders lent their time and money to purchase the necessary land and supplies. Tens of thousands of laborers were hired to complete the huge project. A railroad system called the Central Pacific laid 690 miles (1,110 km) of track that started in Sacramento, California, and ran eastward. Eastern railways connected to a system known as the Union Pacific Railroad. This added 1,087 miles (1,749 km) of track and stretched westward from Council Bluffs, Iowa.

The Central Pacific and Union Pacific were joined at Promontory Summit, Utah, on May 10, 1869. It was a historic moment. Crowds gathered for a big ceremony. A golden spike was driven into the tracks to mark where the two railroads connected. From that point onward, trains carried settlers and supplies westward as the nation expanded to the Pacific coast.

During the rest of the 1800s, innovations in business and marketing helped spread steam power across 19th-century railways. The same was true for diesel-electric systems. But in the century that followed, many travelers chose automobiles over trains. Automobiles allowed drivers to pick their own routes and schedules.

Learning & Innovation Skills

The Transcontinental Railroad couldn't have been completed at a better time. In 1869, America was still recovering from the bloody Civil War (1861–1865), which divided states that supported slavery from those that were against it. Yet work on the railroad involved laborers, businessmen, and politicians from all over the nation. These individuals needed to communicate and collaborate with one another to complete the huge task before them. Besides, what better way to help U.S. citizens feel more connected than to give them a railroad that would allow them to travel across the country?

The railroad industry was faced with the challenge of attracting new passengers.

Freight travel dropped during the Great Depression of the 1920s and 1930s. The Great Depression was an economic crisis that left many Americans poor and without jobs. Railroad companies struggled financially. The Chicago Burlington & Quincy (CB&Q) Railroad began searching for a solution to stay in business. The company's leaders also wanted to improve people's attitudes about passenger service. They came up with the idea to design a passenger train that would amaze Americans with its speed and luxury.

The *Pioneer Zephyr* offered all these things and more. It was sleek, **streamlined**, and could move like a rocket over long distances. It was also crafted from stainless steel, which was lightweight and not likely to rust. The fact that it ran on diesel-electric made it more efficient, too.

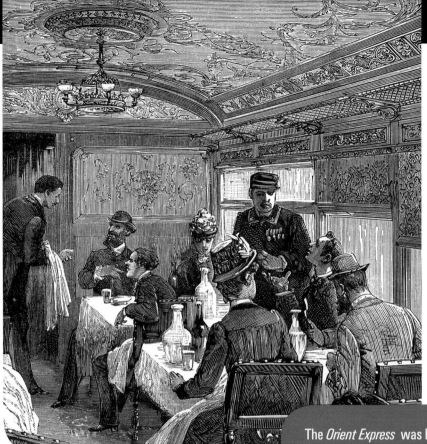

The *Orient Express* was Europe's first international luxury train. It featured beautiful dining cars and excellent service.

The train hit the rails in April 1934. But its unique features alone were not enough to capture public attention. CB&Q businessmen hatched a publicity plan for the following month that would put the *Pioneer Zephyr* in history books. They organized a "Dawn-to-Dusk" dash, in which the train traveled nonstop from Denver, Colorado, to Chicago, Illinois. During the long-distance journey, the *Pioneer Zephyr* moved an average of 78 miles (125 km) per hour. At points along the way, it hit speeds of more than 112 miles (180 km) per hour.

When the *Pioneer Zephyr* arrived in Chicago on May 26, it had covered 1,015 miles (1,633 km) in 13 hours, 4 minutes, and 58 seconds.

No train had ever made such a long, nonstop run in so short a time. The *Pioneer Zephyr* was nicknamed the "Silver Streak." It proved to the public that they could rely on diesel-electric trains to get where they were going in a hurry.

The *Denver Zephyr* trains entered service approximately two years after the *Pioneer Zephyr*.

CHAPTER FOUR

Twenty-First Century Trains

The *Pioneer Zephyr* made people's jaws drop in its day, but trains have come a long way since the 1930s. Railways zigzag on almost every continent and take many forms. New York is famous for its subway trains. Amtrak offers a well-known and widespread U.S. passenger service. Companies all over the world rely on trains to ship their goods in a fast, efficient manner.

Amtrak began offering train service in 1971.

Every year, innovators create new designs that make
trains quicker, cheaper, more comfortable, and able to
haul more weight. Today, people are more concerned
about taking care of the environment than they were
during the last century. Pollution is a major problem.
Diesel-electric trains pollute the air less than steam
locomotives once did. But they still release harmful gases
when their engines burn fuel.

Trains often pass through areas where animals
live. Should railway companies be responsible for
protecting the wildlife near railroads?

Hybrid automobiles are becoming more popular with consumers. Do you think hybrid trains will also catch on?

Some inventors are working on **hybrid** locomotives. Hybrids use fuel, but they mainly rely on battery power to run the train's motors. Scientists continue to work to perfect hybrids. The public supports their development because they would be better for the environment. Today's hybrids, however, cannot compete with fast freight trains that haul a lot of weight. This is because they don't produce as much power as a diesel-electric.

Shanghai, China, was the first city to build and operate a maglev for commercial use.

The train industry is also experimenting with **magnetic** force. This is the force that causes objects made of certain metals to either pull toward each other or push away from one another. Magnetic force is what moves magnetic levitation trains, or maglevs. It is also what causes maglevs to levitate, or float, above the rails. Since maglev trains never actually touch the rails, there is much less friction to slow them down. That means these trains can move at incredibly high speeds.

Maglev trains have been around since the mid-1980s. Scientists in Japan have demonstrated exactly how fast maglevs can move with the *JR-Maglev MLX01*. In 2003, the train clocked in at a record-breaking 361 miles (581 km) per hour! A maglev system also kicked off in China in early 2004. It allows passengers to travel 20 miles (32 km) in 8 minutes.

Maglev trains rely on electricity and magnetic force. They don't pollute the air as much as cars or diesel-electrics, but they are expensive to make. This is partly because they require a special kind of track. Maybe inventors and businessmen will team up to discover new technology that will help make these trains more affordable to run.

CHAPTER FIVE

Problem Solvers Who Set Trains in Motion

Much has changed since horses hauled the earliest trains on wooden rails. The future is certain to bring more changes as today's great minds bring new ideas to train transportation. Here are some of the innovators who relied on critical thinking skills and bright ideas to make trains safer, faster, and more enjoyable.

George Stephenson

George Stephenson was not the first person to experiment with using a steam locomotive. His goal was to make steam power more reliable and efficient. One of his innovations was related to the train's boilers, which are sealed containers in which water is heated to produce steam. The boilers on Stephenson's train were a type that created greater amounts of steam. This innovation

George Stephenson often worked with his son, Robert.

allowed his train, the *Rocket*, to move at a quicker speed over a longer distance. Stephenson, who lived from 1781 to 1848, worked with other inventors and engineers to figure out a design that would help society get the most out of the steam locomotive.

Sleeping cars, such as this one on the Union Pacific Railroad, quickly caught on with passengers.

George Pullman

American inventor George Pullman will always be remembered for designing modern railroad sleeping cars. Before sleeping cars were invented, passengers had to sit upright in uncomfortable wooden seats while traveling on trains. Pullman realized that this was a problem for both the train industry and passengers, especially because train trips often lasted for days. In the mid-1860s, he designed train cars that featured folding beds. By 1867, he had also designed parlor cars and dining cars. Thanks to his innovations, train travel became more appealing to passengers who might otherwise have chosen different forms of transportation.

George Westinghouse

American inventor George Westinghouse realized that safety was a major issue for the railroad industry. Westinghouse lived from 1846 to 1914 and created many inventions, including a life-saving innovation known as the air brake.

Before his invention, workers called brakemen had to turn a massive brake wheel on each car in order to stop the train. They often had to climb across the roof of the train or jump between moving cars—hurrying back and forth—to get to every brake wheel. In addition, early brake systems were sometimes simply not enough to halt trains speeding through steep mountain passes. These limitations resulted in wrecks and other disasters that cost many crew members their lives.

Learning & Innovation Skills

As Pullman cars became more popular, more and more staff were needed to provide services to the guests. Pullman hired many former African American slaves who were looking for jobs after the Civil War. He realized that for his palace cars to really seem like palaces, he would need to hire experienced housekeepers, butlers, and maids. The Pullman Porters saw to passengers' comfort and convenience. It was hard work, but Pullman paid his employees better than what most companies paid African Americans at that time. That made the jobs more appealing to people who were eager to make a better life for themselves.

Other inventors besides Westinghouse had tried to come up with solutions to these tragedies. Yet it was his 1872 version of the air brake that proved the most efficient. Instead of a brake on each car, his design featured a single brake that the engineer controlled. It required less effort to stop a moving train. The air brake was a huge step forward in safety for everyone who rode the rails. Trains could be longer and travel faster thanks to Westinghouse's creative thinking.

Westinghouse was persistent. When his brake model that used steam didn't work, he experimented with air brakes.

Granville Woods

African American inventor Granville Woods lived from 1856 to 1910. He made several improvements to electric railways. One problem with rail travel was that it was impossible for crews on moving trains to communicate with one another and with railway stations. There was no good method of alerting someone if there was an emergency or if a train stopped unexpectedly. Train crews needed a way to let others know that help was needed or to warn nearby trains of a disaster.

In 1887, Woods solved this problem with the aid of a device that already existed, called the **telegraph**. This communication system came before the telephone and used electrical signals to send messages over wires. Woods knew that trains could pick up electrical signals from telegraph lines that ran along the tracks. He developed his version of the induction telegraph in 1887. Trains could finally contact one another and railway stations by exchanging electrical messages.

Glossary

cargo (KAR-go) products or materials that are transported by a train or some other vehicle

efficiency (ee-FISH-uhn-see) the quality of working well without wasting energy

energy (EH-nur-gee) an object's ability to perform work

friction (FRIK-shuhn) a force that is created when two objects rub against one another

fuel (FYOOL) a material such as oil that can be used to produce energy

generator (JEH-neh-ray-tur) a machine used to produce electricity

hybrid (HYE-brid) a type of locomotive that uses a combination of power sources such as fuel and batteries

locomotives (loh-keh-MOH-tivz) vehicles with wheels and an engine that pull a train along tracks

magnetic (mag-NEH-tik) a force that causes objects made of iron to either pull toward each other or push away from one another

publicity (puh-BLIH-seh-tee) promotion or messages designed to make people more aware of a person, product, or idea

streamlined (STREEM-lyned) designed to have a smooth, even shape that creates little resistance against the flow of air

telegraph (TEH-luh-graf) a device that is part of a communication system in which electrical signals are used to send messages over wires

For More Information

BOOKS

Fine, Jil. *The Transcontinental Railroad: Tracks across America*. New York: Children's Press, 2005.

Mayer, Cassie. *By Train*. Chicago: Heinemann Library, 2006.

Zimmermann, Karl. *Steam Locomotives: Whistling, Chugging, Smoking Iron Horses of the Past*. Honesdale, PA: Boyds Mills Press, 2004.

WEB SITES

Baltimore & Ohio Railroad Museum
www.borail.org/
Learn more about the evolution of train technology

Maglev Monorail Pages: Shanghai, China
www.monorails.org/tmspages/MagShang.html
Find out more about maglev monorails in China and around the world

Pioneer Zephyr. Museum of Science and Industry
http://www.msichicago.org/whats-here/exhibits/pioneer-zephyr/
Learn more about the *Pioneer Zephyr*

Index

About the Author

Katie Marsico worked as a managing editor in children's publishing before becoming a freelance writer. She lives near Chicago, Illinois, with her husband and two children. She dedicates this book to her husband, Carl, who is quite an expert on trains.